Letters

to

Jay-Z, Justin Bieber, Chris Brown

& Drake

Signed,

The Illuminati

Cover Art & Designer   Terrence Ford

ISBN-13: 978-0-9911853-1-3
Library of Congress Control Number: 2014936692

To all those who journey on the lighted path—the path of success.

TABLE OF CONTENTS

Letters
to
Jay-Z, Justin Bieber, Chris Brown, & Drake
Signed
The Illuminati

INTRODUCTION

This edition of the *Illuminati Letters Series*, "Letters to Jay-Z, Justin Bieber, Chris Brown, & Drake, Signed The Illuminati," contains letters to a few musical artists and entertainers who either use the name of the Illuminati within their lyrics or are popular in the media. We thank the artists for uplifting the name of Illuminati and we felt that in some small measure they were owed an official response. Since one of our goals is to inspire all persons to walk down the path of the success—the lighted path—the House of Illuminati presents these epistles to these most talented muses in hopes that their example and walk will aid others on their journey of success. Furthermore, it is our hope that these words of wisdom will shed light on the dangers of too much success too soon and how to handle success when one obtains it. Hear ye all our advice to the artists for there is something in it for everyone. Often times, the Illuminati has been mistaken for a dark and evil organization but on the contrary, we are an organization of light and love committed to giving a voice to the people—the voiceless masses who only want to live freely as productive humans on this planet. We are a positive organization and all our letters, no matter how harsh the advice, are written with love. The success of the artists will only benefit the world. Consider how powerful music has been to the generations. Music has the ability to heal the heart and the soul. Music transcends race and has been known to sustain entire clans of people. The ability to sing one's song even in a strange and foreign land has been the glue that held so many together in the times of struggle. In the midst of love, there is music. Our heart-strings and mind-strings can tremble with the sound of a ballad. How many children have been born to the sounds of Motown? Music—sweet music—is the melody that resonates in all of us. The power of music is something that the contemporary muses have taken for granted. These letters not only address their personal matters which have been on public display, but the hope that their light in music will continue to shine.

In addition to Jay-Z, Drake, Chris Brown, and Justin Bieber, we have also included letters to

Miley Cyrus, Common, Queen Latifah, Frank Ocean, Lil Boosie, Kanye West and Wendy Williams. Although it seems as though, we neglect certain musical genres like country and classical, you will discover the reason why as you read the letters. There are no hidden messages in these letters. All readers are encouraged to read the other book written by the Illuminati, "The 66 Laws of the Illuminati: The Secrets of Success" which is available on Amazon.com throughout the world.

Signed,
The Illuminati

Chapter 1

To the Musical Artists

We, the House of Illuminati, would like you to consider the following:

Suppose you were given the opportunity to speak or perform on a stage with a microphone and an audience of 7.2 billion persons from every corner of the world.

What would you say to the people?

What songs would you sing to the masses?

What life would you live as a light and example to those who would follow you?

How much is your light and talent worth?

From this perspective, we begin our discourse with each of you.

Chapter 2

Letter to Justin Bieber

Dear Justin,

The light within you has propelled you on a course of great success. You can go even farther on the path of success if you would just listen to our age-old wisdom. Success can be hard to handle for those who receive it too soon and too quickly. Even for the most seasoned artists and enlightened ones in the business, success can be difficult to handle.

It's hard to witness your private life on public display. It's rough to have every move you make followed by the media or every mistake you make scrutinized by the public eye. You didn't ask to share your life with the world—you just wanted to be the best singer and artist in the industry. Well

8

along with the spotlight of fame comes the personal responsibility to do right and to do good. There is a microscope on your ass with a scope so intense that it detects every imperfection with the greatest magnification. No one expects you to be perfect in the days of your youth, but the world does expect you to act like you have just a little bit of sense.

Here is some advice that should you listen might actually be of some benefit to your journey. We don't want this letter to seem like a lecture but someone needs to guide you for the simple fact that you aren't grown yet. Making money, getting a paycheck, or having a job doesn't make you grown nor does it make you mature. Your brain and your body have not even finished growing. The decisions that you are making just might be the product of an immature and unformed brain. Don't be short-sighted in your desire to live the good life now. We know you are just acting your age but you are doing some harmful things to the longevity of your career.

What's this tale of you allegedly doing drugs—cough syrup and soda drinks? Really? Alleged feuds with neighbors and driving at speeds close to death? C'mon, there must be something better you can do with your body and your time? A million-dollar artist sipping on cough syrup, that's laughable. And that's why so many are laughing at you. You have the resources and the talent to overcome the simple struggles of fame. All these signs could point to a crisis deep within you. You don't have to succumb to silliness. Are these your ideas or is the group of friends you hang out with putting you up to it? How come people around are getting arrested? It can't be "just because they are Black". Could it be because they are engaged in criminal activity? Justin, wise up man and get right.

You are at the crossroads of destroying your name, your image, and your talent unless you like singing behind prison bars. And of these three, your good name is most important. There are no cool points for thuggery in jail. The good news is that it's not too late to put the train back on the track. Here is what you do *(now when you read this, read this with love)*:

First, sit your little ass down somewhere and get your little life together. This should be done alone. Leave your homies alone for a while—they will miss you but they will be there when you return from your journey of soul-searching. Take a trip and travel—Brisbane, Australia; Mobile, Alabama; Rome—find a place rich in history and full of scenic views. Pick a spot along the river's edge and meditate soberly reflecting on what you want to do with your life. Think about that stage with an audience of 7.2 billion people and what you are going to say them. And if that thought overwhelms you, then think about who Justin is on the inside and the desires of your heart. Consider your needs and create a plan for your life. What will you do if the royalties dry up? What will you do if that audience decides to walk out? If you discover that you need rehab or professional mental health treatment during this period, don't be afraid to seek help. This is your time to take care of yourself.

Second, study, study, and study. Go to school! Find a college or university to attend.

Think about Oxford, or Yale, or Stanford. You seem to have a special affinity toward African American culture—so how about you enroll at a Historically Black College or University such as Howard University (like Sean Combs, a.k.a "P. Diddy") or Alabama State University or Morehouse or Fiske. Howard University is just a stone's throw away from the Canadian Embassy seated in the Nation's capital city. Some of the world's greatest musicians like Donny Hathaway, Roberta Flack, Richard Smallwood and Jessye Norman studied in those hallowed halls. Study your craft. Yes, God has given you a gift of greatness, but you run the risk of destroying that gift and the light within you. Can you see yourself going to class, studying with good students, training with great professors, and singing with the best? As with every college student, we expect that you would have a bit of fun along the way, party, and experiment with love. But leave the drugs and self-medication alone. Keep a sober head about you at all times and enjoy the experience of enlightenment. You owe yourself to study! Treat yourself to an education. And while you are there, stop by Andrew Rankin Chapel at Howard or King Chapel at Morehouse and feed your spiritual self. Immerse yourself in the positive elements of the culture which speaks to your heart and soul. Learn all that you can in order to be the best that you can.

Third, find a cause or an issue to which you can commit. Find an issue in which you are passionate about. Find a cause to which you want to lend your voice and your service. Make this cause a priority and invest yourself in making the world a better place through your devotion. It all sounds so utopian but instead of making the news for something negative like speeding in an overpriced car, make history for changing the lives of so many in a positive way. Do you know how many people need clean water, textbooks for school, libraries, a fuel source to cook their food, access to the digital age—so many ways that you can make a significant difference?

Finally, you can't do it all by yourself. Once you have retreated, collected your thoughts, and returned to your normal grind, you will need some loving and positive people around you—and we are not talking about the homies. We understand the need to have peers and friends that you can trust. But we are talking about a family-figure like a grandmother who will throw her loving arms around you and hug you and hold you. Every person on this earth needs love and at some point in their life a little help too. We love you and only want the best for you. Do good and do well.

Thankfully, it's not too late to make a change. There is still time to make a positive difference in this world for you are yet still a child. We know it sounds like a tall order but don't let it overwhelm you. Learn how to use the power to influence. You can lead a generation if you get yourself together. Walk in the light, where the dew drops of mercy shine bright.

Signed,
The Illuminati

Chapter 3

Letter to Wendy Williams

Dear Wendy,

How you doing...?

Wendy, you are a phenomenal woman and clearly a loving mother. You are the awesome mother of a teenager—thank God for the arrival of the teenage years. We can hear the sigh of a million mothers who will read this. So we write to you and the millions of mothers who find themselves in a similar situation—caring for a teenage adolescent youth.

Even more thanks to God that you aren't doing it alone. There are so many single moms in the world today who struggle from sun-up to sun-down just to make ends meet—left alone, for whatever reason, as the sole bearer of responsibility for the growth and development of another human life. In some cases, even if the father is the breadwinner, the burden of care stills falls on the backs and breasts of the mother. With humor, then along came Similac and helped a lot of folk out. But such is life. Childrearing is ordained by the Creator and one of the most blessed obligations that a person can undertake.

Wendy, by now, thousands and thousands have watched your emotional display of love for your son. It was ten seconds of time that resonated long after the last tear dried. The source of which could have been the combination of many things the obvious hormones, time of day, the weather, hurt feelings, wounded ego, and the list goes on. No one really knows but one thing is for sure: there is nothing like a mother's love.   Love can be a tricky thing for love often hurts the ones who care the most.

You have the difficult task of raising an African American teenage son in America.   Make no comparison to the culture of your home and the home of Madonna. Those two worlds have a totally different set of realities. There is so much that you have to prepare your young man to meet in the next five years when the world says to him, "Hello, let's play for real." For example, if your son were to hang out with Justin Bieber, we can guarantee he would probably go to jail; or if he were to sit in a car in Florida with the music blaring, his chances of meeting the undertaker increases two fold; or if he walks from the local 7-11 with a hoodie through a neighborhood with a mentally warped street captain, he might not make it to his final destination. There are some hard realities that face your son that overrides any internal desire for him to like or idolize you. You are fighting against some statistics that are going to take all the love you got.

A mother only wants the best for her child. As a result, mothers tend to develop a certain need for control that the teenage child makes it his or her job to defy. Dads often get a pass—rarely when a child grows up and becomes socially awkward do they say, "Didn't your father teach you good manners?" Most of the time, the question is, "Didn't your mother teach you manners?" So worry not about being his friend, it is okay if you are viewed as a bad guy. Sometimes you have to be a bad guy in order to make sure that he becomes a good guy.

As a parent, it's hard when you fuss and it seems like what you said went into one ear and came out the other. It's hard when your parental orders go ignored—and you see those socks on the floor in the same spot for two weeks straight or the dishes stack up in the sink or the trash that you decreed to leave the house sits there idle. Whereas, Dad can speak one word and it seems like the kid couldn't move any faster to fulfill the request. On one hand, the kid wants to please his father and wants to be seen as a buddy—as cool as it seems, the father-son relationship can be quite fragile. He knows in his heart, that no matter what he does or how nasty he acts, his mother is going to love him—because that's what a mother is supposed to do, love her child no matter what.

This role of mother is so important that the Son of God even had one. God wanted his Son to have a mother for no human on earth—no matter how divine—can make it without one. This mother of His pushed him out in a manger, so the story goes; cheered for him at all his sermons, cried out for him at a trial, and wept for him at the sight of his fatal wounds. And like the poet Khalil Gibran penned in his poem, "On Children," he wrote:

> And a woman who held a babe against her bosom said, "Speak to us of Children."
> And he said:
> Your children are not your children.
> They are the sons and daughters of Life's longing for itself.
> They come through you but not from you,
> And though they are with you, yet they belong not to you.
> You may give them your love but not your

thoughts.

For they have their own thoughts.

You may house their bodies but not their souls,

For their souls dwell in the house of tomorrow,

which you cannot visit, not even in your

dreams.

You may strive to be like them, but seek not to

make them like you.

For life goes not backward nor tarries with

yesterday.

You are the bows from which your children as

living arrows are sent forth.

The archer sees the mark upon the path of the

infinite, and He bends you with His might that

His arrows may go swift and far.

Let your bending in the archer's hand be for

gladness;

For even as he loves the arrow that flies, so He

loves also the bow that is stable.

Wendy, the fact of the matter is that you and

your son probably have a normal, great relationship.

He loves you more than he can even express or

comprehend. Remember we teach our children how

to love. And with most children, they probably take

their mother's love for granted. To him, you will

always be his mother no matter how pissed you may

be or how loud you fuss—you are just mom, the divine caretaker of the seed of greatness.

So to all the mothers: be encouraged, stay encouraged, and as the hymnologist suggests, "sometimes you have to encourage yourself." Keep on loving, keep on fussing, and keep on fighting for their future. Realize that you can't always control your children and they do have a mind of their own—an unformed, immature, and often stubborn mind, but a mind nonetheless. It's your job to teach them how to walk but when they walk and how far they walk is not always up to you.

Children grow. They go through different phases in life—each with its own unique challenge. Sometimes a mother can love her child too much. Her love smothers the life of her child. We only mention that as a caveat to some mothers out there. Love your child but love them in healthy way.

In the final analysis, your son is blessed and privileged to have you, Wendy Williams, as his mother.

Not just the strong Wendy Williams that we see on television, but the Wendy that Thomas and Shirley raised—the Wendy that perseveres through all odds, the Wendy that has believed in herself and won't give up. And most importantly, the Wendy that will love him no matter what—when the world mounts against him, when two or three girlfriends (or significant others) have left him, or when society dejects him—a mother that tried her best to be the best mother she could.

Wendy, we love you and we love every mother on earth.

Signed,
The Illuminati

Chapter 4

Letter to Miley Cyrus

Dear Miley,

Looks like you turned out to be a beautiful woman—a sexy woman. (Before the feminists and sociologists take up a sea of arms, we are not objectifying Miley based upon her body and physical appeal. But if that's what Miley is selling, we might as well get that out of the way early on.). Miley, you have had an interesting journey of development and we are certain that you remain on the path of self-discovery. It's amazing how much you have grown and changed over the years. It's almost as if you have reinvented yourself. The remnants of your character, "Hannah Montana," are fading away. But in reality, "Hannah Montana," is not real, it was a character in which you portrayed. Some people seem to have a hard time separating you from your character.

Your musical gifts are exceptional and superb. Continue to develop your talent to the highest potential possible. Your "twerk" skills need some work though. Like we told Justin, go to college. Send a message to girls around the world that education is important. Let them know that the pursuit of higher knowledge is a cool thing and a worthwhile venture. We are aware that you said it's something that you would pursue later in life. And we can respect that only if you hold true to your word. It would be hard to hold down a million dollar music career and go to school at the same time. So we understand that at this point in your life you are choosing your career. You are smart

28

and positioning yourself to live freely and independently. That's what most of us desire—to live as we choose.

Miley, young lady, discover who you are. Learn as much about yourself as you can so that you can be genuine and authentic to the calling within. If you choose to use your good looks and sex appeal to sell records, that's your decision. And if you can live with yourself for doing so, then that's your right. Earn as much as you can now, so that you don't have to work so hard later on life—those looks won't last. We know that you aren't all about the money—your driving force is personal freedom. The ability to do you and be you is what motivates you and that's alright too.

So don't worry about the haters. The haters do what they do best—hate. Love them because they care so much about you. They only serve to increase your media sales. Be you!!! If they are mad because you left Disney, so what? If you want short blonde hair, so what? If you want to let your tongue hang out of your mouth like a dog in heat, who cares? You are an adult now and you can be whatever you want to be so long as you are responsible. Just be responsible—remember you have a microphone with an audience of 7.2 billion people. There are little girls who admire you. There are people who love you. Your message can't be that it's okay to do drugs and it's okay to use your body for monetary benefits though. You can't prostitute your blessing. Your talent is a gift from the Creator—use it wisely and use it for good.

Uplift those who are coming behind you, and find an issue that you can devote your time toward solving. Be free but be responsibly free.

You are at the beginning of a great career—no need to mess it up. But for some reason we believe that you know what you are doing. Your career can take either of two paths—short or long.

If you feel that your career will be short then earn as much as you can now so that you can enjoy life in your later years.

If you desire a long career, then definitely don't mess it up with silly activity. Show love to your people and nothing else will matter. Overall, make your career and your life significant. Your music can be powerful.

Above all, we love you for being you.

Signed,
The Illuminati

Chapter 5

Letter to Chris Brown

Dear Christopher,

Remember the stage upon which you stand while you sit in the prison cell due to actions of your own hand. You have an audience of billions, what are you saying unto them?

Chris, you are too talented to be in jail, even though the jailhouse is full of some of the most talented individuals on earth. Not only are you too talented, but you are too intelligent to squander your gifts. How come you couldn't just chill out in that rehabilitation facility for a few weeks and just rest or work on your spiritual and mental space?

Many of us ponder the reasons that have led you down the path of self-destruction. Is there any reason you can name for fighting members of the public, the press, or the paparazzi? Can you think of any other way to handle civil disputes other than resorting to physical arms, violent outbursts, and fighting? Yea, yea, we don't want you to be abused or disrespected. Those are legitimate concerns. However, you shouldn't put yourself in a position of powerlessness by trying to prove how strong you are. You will always lose a physical fight with someone on the street even if you are the winner. You have more resources, therefore, you will be perceived as the bully even if you are provoked. Use your mind, not your fists—walk away. The problem with anger management or any strong emotion is its ability to override the rational mind.

Even in the moment where you feel as though you are gaining control, you have often already lost control. In those cases, especially where there is a clear exit, it is best to leave quickly to preserve your own safety. In simple words, just get the hell out of there. More than likely you shouldn't have been in the situation from the start.

The reality of the matter is that if you weren't a talented young artist with an abundance of resources, statistics show that you probably would have already been in jail. It's a sad fact—it's an American fact. You can hire people, like a security team, to protect you while in public and keep the riffraff away. Now in private settings, like with Rihanna, you are left up to your own self-will and internal locus of control to subdue your passions and restrain yourself. She may have deserved whatever may have transpired in the car on that night but was that outcome the only alternative? We can't change the past but we can think better in the future. Now to your defense, matters of the heart have a way of clouding the judgment of the mind. The damage of these events often last far beyond the few minutes which caused them. Which brings us to another point: life is more than episodic events. So everybody needs to get over the Chris Brown-Rihanna situation—it's old.

We live in a world where second chances are possible. You have the power and ability to overcome past situations and turn them into positive moments. Like we have told all of your peers, pick a cause that enlivens you, and put your energy into making the world a better place. Imagine if you were to set up studios around the nation, or partner with a few high schools in places like Chicago or Detroit, or teach a master class in music production at Howard University or somewhere deep down in the South like the Communications Department at Alabama State University. Imagine the significant contribution that you can make to the lives of others beyond the stage. Educate folk; give your time to the less fortunate not the State. Juxtapose that experience with sitting in a jail cell.

What made you seek to become a musical artist? What made you want to take the mic on the stage and sing your song? Are you living within your purpose? Listen for the call of the voice within you. Find your way along the path of success. Let the light within you carry you forth on the journey. But in order for you to do this, you have to commit yourself to learning about yourself and loving yourself enough to not destroy who you are. Let the violence go, it is impairing your success. You can be a man without violence.

Some of your greatest moments will come out of adversity. Use all that you have towards developing your gifts, your talents, and your personality. Eliminate any and all drug activity if present—it's okay to "turn up" every now and then but during this period of meditative contemplation, cleanse your mind and your body. Seek help for any problem that is bigger than you can handle— just seek help. Sit down with someone and let the process work. It's just a few short weeks but it can help you over a lifetime. Honor your essence—be real but in being real, don't be stupid.

Chris, we want to see you succeed. You can turn this around. We want you to have a long career. Our greatest fear is that if you continue down your current route, your career will end before its time. The people will not support you if you continue to act a fool or can't pull your life together, no matter how talented you are. Do good man! Be good man! No matter how hard the climb may be up the rough side of the mountain, you can do it. Everyone has personal battles—deal with your struggles and get well before coming back to public performance.

Your career demands that you be well and whole. You can overcome the negative publicity and the only way to do that is to do good. This is a pivotal point in your professional career—decide if you wish to go on and how you wish to go on. You are young and you want to participate in the fun

39

activities of your youth—we understand all that. Just do it smartly. A millionaire should not be engaged in a street fight—just saying. Does that even make sense to you? Just come back healthy and strong, with a clear understanding of your mission and purpose. Earn as much money to support your years in retirement. Take care of your future today!

And then, discover how you are going to help others. Be a message as you take back the mic on the stage before the audience. Your life is in your hands—be about the business of doing good and an education won't hurt either.

Signed,
The Illuminati

Chapter 6

Letter to Drake

Dear Drake,

Medusa heads and Illuminati? We thank you for the mention in your rap song, unlike Kanye West, who we could do without. His success remains a mystery to us. So many artists in your genre of music misinterpret and misrepresent the Illuminati in their lyrics. Illuminati is not an organization composed of only those who can afford Versace—although many of us could but rarely would we waste money on expensive fabrics when we know the real value of cotton. We digress because we didn't write you to talk about Greek mythology, the rise and fall of cotton, nor the insignificance of Kanye West (Is there a cause for which he stands?).

Illuminati is an organization dedicated to obtaining power for the people and by the people. We have fought and we continue fight for fair power distribution of the people. Wherever there is great disparity among the haves and the have-nots, there we are. We are like the Robin Hoods of the powerful few—we take power from the powerful and redistribute that power back to the hands of the people. We are a people's party. We love the people and we want all people around the world to be successful—all people!

Drake, you are one of the most talented lyricists on the musical scene today. Your art is more than a profession, it's a vocation. You are living out your calling to highest and we value the work that you produce. But we challenge you on two issues: poverty and brotherhood.

If we could give you an issue to tackle, it would be poverty. Do you realize that you have the power to be the ambassador for the poor and impoverished around the world? You can be the champion for world hunger. We could have picked any rap artist who uses the name of Illuminati in their lyrics but we chose you. We chose you because your intelligent command of the English language propels you above the rest of the field. Use that intelligence to speak on behalf of the millions who go to sleep at night without a good meal. Use that intelligence to figure out how to get clean drinking water to the remotest villages of Africa. Use that intelligence to figure out how to make sure that every child has access to nutritious fruits and vegetables.

We applaud you for the work that you have done with high school students by putting a music studio in an educational facility. Drake, can you replicate this? Can you partner with others to help empower the youth? Music is so important to the development of the mind. If you strengthen the youth, you can strengthen the future of the republic.

On the issue of brotherhood, give Chris Brown a call. Tell him that you are there with him (not for him, but with him) if he should ever need you. Strengthen one another. And if he declines your presence, then at least you tried. Be a bridge for reconciliation. Let them see you function in the realest since of brotherhood. In the process you will discover that old enemies can become "new friends."

Remember when you grab the mic to speak to every young brother and every young man, encourage them to get on the lighted path. Light up with the power of education! Light up with brotherly love! Light up with the hope of a better tomorrow! Tell them how to travel down the lighted path without the use of drugs or other foreign substances. Propel them on the lighted path of success. Help them as much as you can. Travel to any place that will accept your presence, any place that you can make a difference, and speak to the youth. Tell them to put down their swords and guns and pick up a book. Tell them to learn trades that will lead to their self-development. Speak on the matters of race and discrimination where it matters the most. Be a poet and a prophet for the ages, not just for the profits. Make whatever you do matter. Consider teaming up with Common or Russell Simmons on projects to advance causes that matter to the people.

Finally, our Brother, take time to strengthen the weak. Don't let your personal catfights cause us to lose the war. Use all your gifts and talents for good. You stand in a special place in the minds and hearts of the youth. Be responsible to their care.

Signed,
The Illuminati

Chapter 7

Letter to Common and Queen Latifah

Dear Common and Queen Latifah,

We applaud and congratulate both of you for your positive messages and continual desire to uplift others. In addition to that, we write to also challenge you both to be spokespersons for causes that will and can impact the youth of the United States and the world.

Common, the work that you have done for the cause of peace is remarkable. Continue to hold peace summits even when it is not popular. The children in urban American cities are killing one another, adults in various places are shooting teenagers while "standing their ground," and unnecessary wars are killing thousands without end. The cause of peace is one of the noblest efforts that one can engage. Peace is possible if we learn how to settle our differences through diplomacy and dialogue.

When you speak, you give voice to the voiceless, become a friend to the friendless, and provide power for the powerless. You can make a difference in the lives of the youth. They will work with you, if you work with them. Seek to understand the issues which cause the youth to commit violence and then speak on their behalf. No child should fear going to school. The schoolhouse should be one of the safest places in their lives. Work with the Mayor, the Secretary of Education, and the President to address these issues. Both of you should work with Oprah to advance these causes.

Queen Latifah ("Dana Owens"), you are the living embodiment of a phenomenal and beautiful woman. Congratulations on your new show and we know that your success will be long. As a music artist, your talent is remarkable but as a communicator, you are even greater. Queen, you personify positivity. The world should take note of you. Have you considered teaching others the art of communication? Have you ever considered a future in politics? Any organization would be both proud and lucky to have you as a spokesperson.

Now let us ask you, are there any causes on which you have been silent which your voice would have added power? You have played it safe thus far along your journey. But your image does not need protecting anymore. You have proved yourself to be a great human being. It's time that we hear from you on a few issues—gender equality for one. Don't be afraid to get your hands dirty. Love will always overcome any amount of hate.

Common and Queen Latifah, thank you for being two examples of great human beings. Your conscientiousness warrants attention. Let us hear your voices! Continue to love the people and all else will follow.

Signed,
The Illuminati

Chapter 8

Letter to Jay-Z

Dear Mr. Carter,

We greet you as an elder statesman. We appeal to your sensibilities as a senior member of the musical arts community. You have enjoyed a long, successful, and prosperous career—so much so that many confuse your achievements with membership in the Illuminati. Once again, we thank you for your letter posted on the Facebook medium in which you denounced any affiliation with Illuminati. *(We presume the letter was from you.)* Your achievements are the product of your own hard work. We applaud your ingenuity and entrepreneurial accomplishments. Once upon a time in the not too distant decade, some musicians were paid pennies on a record but this we know will not ever be you. You have progressively advanced your talents and career to secure your future very well.

We also know that you are very philanthropic and committed to several causes without any public notoriety. Your foundation awards educational scholarships, no matter how small in comparison to your net worth; this is commendable. We are sure if you could do more in donating to your foundation as well as other education organizations that you would do so.

Either way, Mr. Carter, creating educational endowments and contributing to educational pursuits are critical to the perpetuation of a great society. Toward that end, we challenge you to partner with Wynton Marsalis to assist music programs in New Orleans to train and educate the youth on how to play an instrument. Can you work with bands—raw musical talent—and ensure that they have instruments to create the wonderful sound of music? Can you put some electronic studios in schools in the poorest of neighborhoods? Can you teach a class at a university on hip-hop culture in the American society? Do you feel as though you have a responsibility to give back? It's okay if you answer, "No." Perhaps if you answered, "No," then we could understand your choice to keep silent. As we consider Muhammad Ali, Harry Belafonte, Sidney Poitier—we must ask, "Where is your voice?" Are the times so different that successful musical artists feel no need to make a contribution to the social ills of the world?

In every time, a prophet speaks. Your poetry drips with discourse on the politics of society. Your lyrics give us insight into the plight of your people in the American context. Yet, your presence is absent on the battlefield of concern. Is there a cause for which you can speak? We saw you at a Trayvon Martin rally and your presence spoke volumes. On so many issues, your voice could actually make a difference. Dr. Michael E. Dyson teaches a class at Georgetown University where he highlights your contributions to the landscape of American culture. He compares your muses and rhymes with the poetry of likes of Thoreau. We happen to agree with his critical assessment, yet, how does that translate to social justice and community action? Stand up man! We don't need another talking head—society and your people need your voice to tilt the scales of power just a little bit in their favor. Or did Barney's pay for silence?

If we speak clearly about the matter, you have used your craft for the accumulation of capital and profit. Capitalism is a great thing but don't forget your community. It's the money of your supporters that allows you to live comfortably. We don't want this letter to get too heavy but what exactly are you selling Mr. Carter? The Christian Bible warns folk about gaining the world and losing their soul. Don't prostitute the blessing of your gift and don't sell out. Never forget where you came from and never forget who you are and whose you are.

Even within the industry, take some of the younger artists under your wing. Advise them on how to handle success. Sit them down and instruct them on the lighted path. Mentorship builds community. And where there is community, there is always capital. Strengthen the young and conquer all the problems of society. Teach the young musicians the power of music. Tell them how music was utilized by groups like NWA or Public Enemy or KRS One. Recall the effect that music had on your parents' generation. Educate them on B.B. King, Muddy Waters, and James Brown. Music can be a powerful medium—it can tell the history of a people and often convey their struggle and their protest. Call Wynton tonight and put your body on the battlefield to save the youth.

Do we expect that you would act like an elder statesman?

Yes, we expect it but will you?

Signed,
The Illuminati

Chapter 9

Letter to Torrence Hatch aka Lil Boosie

Dear Lil Boosie,

Sit tight. Remember that the system already has its fangs in you and will not stop biting. The system will try to bite you at every turn...again and again...then again. It'll go so far as to cut the road off to demolish the bridge toward your success.

Your fans looking forward to your shows and concerts in other states will still be there six months from now if they are truly loyal fans of the musical gift you have been given to share with the World. Be wise with your words and careful in all your actions. One mistake can end it all. Keep in mind that the fans—the people—are not in love with you but rather your gift. Therefore, uplift the gift over the man (Torrence Hatch) and success will follow.

In the meantime, look at your own grass, because snakes dwell closer to us than we think. You have received wise counsel from California all the way to Florida. Be sure to look for these counselors that have supported you through the incarceration process because now that you are free many others are looking to join the "Boosie Band Wagon." Be wise in your steps from now into the future. Share with your fans, many of which are young black men and black teenagers, the actual finer things in life: love, freedom and family. Nice cars are merely expensive pieces of metal, and all the fine women leave after the director says, "Cut!"

Self-edification through reading, learning, and studying should be the aim of young men. Self-creation by writing, producing and innovating should be the goals of young men. Share this and the lessons you have learned before your incarceration, throughout it and now that you are free. Don't tell them why education is important, show them. Show them the books you have read, and the lessons you have studied, and why you earned your G.E.D while incarcerated. Let them know that your gift comes from dedication and practice and from discipline and due diligence. Rap about the streets and the realities of the unfairness of life, but hold your fans accountable. For what reason is there to harm my neighbor that I played with as a boy because today he lives on a different street or is part of a different team? The reality of violence in communities—especially some communities of color, communities of black people—.is senseless. Speak about it...speak truth to power, but challenge everyone to do better. The ball is in your court again...what will you do with it?

A wise man once said, "When it feels like the world is on my shoulders, I look at my pictures from when I was free and it gives hope and determination to keep on pushing." We hope you listen to this wise man...his name was Torrence Hatch aka Lil Boosie. Sometimes you have to encourage yourself to reach the top of the mountain.

Signed,
The Illuminati

Chapter 10

Letter to Frank Ocean

Dear Mr. Ocean,

"Freedom is what I seek, and in seeking that freedom, my grandest fear is to be dismembered from the body of those who love me because they will actually know who 'I' really am," is a quote written by a member of the House of Illuminati ages ago.

You, Frank, have faced this question in one of the most hardened industries (besides politics) on the planet—the Hip-Hop Industry. The industry has seemingly become a field where image is king, narcissism is the norm, and thuggism, materialism, sexism, homophobia and hate have replaced an art born out of a need to express the realities of a resilient people who fought tooth and nail to survive in these United States of America. An art that used to be expressed through poetry in motion which demonstrated love, affection, dissatisfaction, and life through word and rhyme—what really has Hip-Hip become?

It is in knowing this that we quiver at how Hip-Hop, an art created through the voice of the minority, has become a perpetrator of hate and oppression towards other minority groups—women and homosexuals.

It should not have made news that you "came out," because the LGBT community has always been a part of the entertainment industry. LGBT persons have always been amongst the people. Have you ever heard of Little Richard?

From music icons such as Little Richard to the Civil Rights Movement pioneers such as Bayard Rustin and literary giants like James Baldwin, one can presume that LGBT persons have always been a part of the scene.

Frank, just know that any backlash you receive as a result of your choice to reveal who you are comes from a place of insecurity in others...often a fear that they can't do what you do, often from the reality that they struggle with the fact they are just like you. And so it follows: anti-abortionists that go as far as to murder abortion doctors and people who hate gays secretly hate themselves, are often themselves homosexual. Realize you are not alone in your struggle and no one ever is—whatever it might be.

This may or may not be your cause, only you know that, but we ask that you continue to lead by example and continue honing your craft because letting your light shine gives others affirmation to do the same.

Now at the same time, do not define yourself solely on the basis of your sexuality. Sexuality plays such a small part in the human experience. It should not be the lens by which a person views. If this happens, a person will miss out on so much of God's creation. Who you love or what you love can come in so many forms—even a woman. Go to the microphone and speak to the world.

Signed,
The Illuminati

Chapter 11

Letter to Kanye West

Dear Kanye,

    Who are you and what have you done

lately?

Signed,
The Illuminati

Chapter 12

Letter to all Those who Seek Fame

To all those who seek Fame:

Be careful for what you wish. Fame is not for everybody and everybody is not for fame. Matter of fact, do not even seek fame but instead just seek to be great. How does one become great, you ask? The Christian scriptures suggest that those who wish to be great should become servants. Everyone can be great because everyone can serve. So instead of seeking fame, seek to serve humanity. And when you seek to serve, along the journey of your service one will experience greatness.

We have heard many of the youth say, "I want to be famous." What is it about fame that you really desire? Do you desire the world to know your name? Do you desire to be known by everyone? Do you desire to lose your privacy and be on public display? If any of those are your desires then, fame is not for you.

Abandon your ambition to be famous and do everything you can do to increase your ability. If you become great at your craft, the world will find you. Your gifts and talents will make room for you in the world. If you are good at singing and happen to live in Chicago, the people in China will hear about you. If you dance well in London, people in Los Angeles will know who you are. If in New York, you paint like the masters, people in New Zealand will seek to see your work. Instead of fame, just be the best at your artistic craft. If there is anything that the Illuminati could impress upon all those who seek fame, it is not to seek fame.

Discover the light within you—find your purpose and mission in life. Learn as much as you can about yourself before you embark upon your path. Learn those things that you will accept and those things that you will not accept. Be faithful to the divine within you. Always listen to the call of the Creator within in you. Establish your moral center and make concrete your character. Be the best you that you can be—authentic and real. And when you open your mouth, or use your hands, you will pour yourself out. Only until you have done these things will you be ready to set out on the path of success. Success is possible to everyone. Be loving, kind, and humble—always. Don't stray too far from lighted path.

Success must be managed. Too much too soon can destroy you. Having too much power before you are able to handle it can be deadly. How can you manage a million dollars, if you have trouble keeping up with a hundred dollars? In order to handle fame, one must have a firm grasp on who you are. This should be a non-negotiable element of fame. We can make you famous, but unless you are grounded, you will be destroyed. Those who earn success, enjoy it longer. Work hard on your talents, and success will follow.

Maybe it's fortune or money that you desire? We understand that as well. After all, your craft is your career. It's okay to seek a wage for your labor. But never prostitute your blessing! Never use the light within you strictly for capital gains. Truly, you can gain the world and lose your soul, lose your self, and lose your way. Fame is not worth that. Rarely have we ever found a tombstone which read: "Here lies a famous person." Every artist has to eat, live, and survive but the pursuit of your craft should to be fulfill your passion, not to obtain a paycheck. The paycheck will come if you are good at what you do.

Music has the power to move nations. Music has the power to soothe the soul and console the mind. Music is the historian's friend and the sociologists ally. It captures the mood of a time and tells the story of the struggle. Music can be a weapon that can pierce the heart. When we celebrate, there is music. When we console our loved ones, there is music. When we carry our dead to the grave, there is music. When we participate in the creation process, there is music. Where would the world be if King David had not assured that the psalmist made a written record of his or her lyrics?

Consider the power of music in the nonviolent movements for change. It was music that made the struggle bearable. Society needs music. Society needs art. To any person who has the gift of art—not just music but the creative force for art—you are blessed by the Creator to be a blessing to others.

The Illuminati is dedicated to ensuring that all persons are successful. Toward that goal, we recommend that you read, "The 66 Laws of the Illuminati: The Secrets of Success." (which is available on Amazon.com throughout the world). To those who seek success, we wish you speed on the path of self-discovery.

With love.

Signed,
The Illuminati.

Get a copy of

"The 66 Laws of the Illuminati:

The Secrets of Success"

Available worldwide on Amazon.com!

www.amazon.com

www.ingramcontent.com/pod-product-compliance
Lightning Source LLC
Chambersburg PA
CBHW020643130626
46552CB00003B/1384